AF445318

Happily Ever Afters,

Slaying Dragons,

& Other Sleights of Hand

Happily Ever Afters, Slaying Dragons, and
Other Sleights of Hand A Poetry Collection
By K.A. Moore by Kindle Direct Publishing.

©2020 K.A. Moore

All rights reserved. No portion of this book
may be reproduced in any form without
permission from the publisher, except as
permitted by U.S. copyright law. For
permissions contact:

k.a.mooreauthor@gmail.com

Cover by Enrique Meseguer
https://pixabay.com/images/id-4070966/

To the dreamers, warriors, and survivors.
May you always remember just how
strong you are.

And to Adina,
You are the star in my darkness.

Chapters

Table of Contents

Trigger warning:

Some of the material contained within deals with sexual assault, child abuse, and trauma.

Please practice self-care before, during, and after reading, as it can affect even the sturdiest of readers.

Thank you for deciding to take this journey with me.

-K.A. Moore

Surprise

The victim recognizes what is happening
and becomes afraid.
It is difficult for the victim to make sound
because it is a struggle to breathe.

There was lightning in your eyes
The day I met you,
And I knew a storm was brewing.
I just didn't know
How widespread
The devastation would be.

-You haunt me still

And they lived happily ever after,
Except they didn't.
How can they live happily ever after
When he was expecting Cinderella,
And got Sleeping Beauty?
How can happy happen when his dreams
are
Put on display
And her dreams become ashes in her
mouth?
They told her 'happy is a decision'
but never told her
That no matter how often she chooses
happy,
she'd be left
With disappointment.
He dreams of the wife he wanted when he
married her,
But never got.
Is still waiting all these years later.
She dreams of a boy across the ocean,
With bourbon colored eyes, and a smile
Painted on by the devil.
His voice as smooth as a shot of whiskey.
She's never met him, but puts her hopes in
the idea of him.
Of what he could be.
But that's too much pressure for an
imaginary person to lift.
So she stays in her head where it's safe.
No one can harm her here.
No one will harm her if she creates them
all.
She lives in her head,
he lives in the real world,
And as the years pass,
they pass each other,
Until they're strangers.

Until one kiss breaks the sleep she's in.
And they live happily ever after…

-And repeat

He was her everything.
She was just something to pass his time.
From the time they met, it was always him
before her:
his dream,
his passions,
his way.
She followed along,
hope upon hope
that he would see her,
see inside to her silent screams.
His love smothered her like a flame held
underwater,
and nothing he said or did ever saved her.
She was drowning from the inside out,
never one to ask for help,
just hoped that someone would see her
 disappear beneath the waves inside.
On the outside she seemed fine,
always one to have a smile on her face.
She was the ultimate actress
because no one caught on.
She jumped from thing to thing,
place to place,
person to person
to try to stop the waves from cresting over
her head.
In the end,
she sunk deep beneath the waves
and disappeared.
Everything flitted away like smoke from
the end of a cigarette,
drawn to the sky
and carried away by the wind.
By the time he realized anything was
wrong,
she was long gone.
The vibrant girl he fell in love with

had long since drowned.
In her place was an empty shell,
like the shells that litter the beach
as the waves crash against the shore.
All she wanted was love like the heroines
in her books:
the all-consuming love that devoured and
created,
that could destroy the universe
as easily as it could build cities of
skyscrapers.

What she got was a fleeting fancy that
barely boiled.
As she drowned,
he held her hand
and let her go
when she needed him most.
As the years passed,
he poured his all into everything he did
and wondered why she didn't do the
same.
The smiles were automatic,
the words the best she could do.
When he finally recognized what went
wrong,
she was just another song of the seas.

-He never did like sailing

All you ever do is try to snuff out my light.
What you forget is
I am a raging inferno.
I refuse to dim my light,
Simply because you are required to squint.

- I suppose sunglasses are in order

Be careful with my heart
The stitches are worn
From all the times
I had to put it back together
Just to keep myself from
Falling apart.

-The thread still frays

People say
there's no such thing as ghosts,
But I know that's not true.
The memory of us still haunts me
Every time I close my eyes.

-Are you apparition or human?

I'll probably write about you for the rest of
my life.
There won't be a pen stroke
That doesn't have you wrapped in it
somehow.
No line of laughter
No smiled described
That won't have you somewhere in it.
But your legacy is the nightmares you left
behind for me
And how I'll write my way out of the hell
you left me in
Broken and unwanted.
I'll probably write about you for the rest of
my life,
But only because it will take that long
For me to banish you from my system.

-How much longer must I bleed for you?

I'm drowning
And you're standing three feet away
Yelling "learn how to swim".
Like I'm not frantically trying
To keep my head above the water.
Like the waves aren't wrapped tight,
Shoving wet tendrils down my throat.
That by reaching out your hand
I'll pull you under too.
I'm not asking you to save me,
I'm asking you to lend a hand.
To pull me closer
So my feet can touch.
To give me a shred of hope
That I can do this on my own.
Instead you disappear when I need you
most
And wonder why my insides have turned
to ice.
Why my words are not words
But drops of water.
Why my skin is like an anchor
Pulling me beneath the waves.
What good is knowing how to swim
If you know you'll never reach the shore?

-And this is only the first act

1. It does not go how I planned it in my
    head.
    There is no bedspread covered in
    rose petals, each one signifying the
    depth of his love for me.
    There aren't candles scattered across
    the room, casting a soft glow to ease
    my nerves.
    The wind isn't whispering through
    the window, blowing open his shirt
    to reveal his washboard abs, like the
    covers on my mom's smutty novels
    that I'd been sneaking for the past
    few months.
    There isn't an angel chorus singing as
    two bodies become one flesh.

2. My soundtrack is the drunken
    giggling coming from the other room
    as my brother seduces my best
    friend,
    because I couldn't bring a friend
    around he wouldn't hit on,
    which strangely enough is why I
    stopped bringing them around.
    Why I stopped being close to anyone
    who thought that was okay, and
    enjoyed it.

3. The only illumination comes from the
    streetlight outside of the second-story
    window,
    which sounds more like the
    beginning of a horror story than a
    love story.
    Which, I suppose, fits much better
    now that I think about it.
    Because doesn't skeleton branch

hands reaching for the sky under the
light of the autumn moon,
fit much better to a night I want to
forget and can't help but remember?
Fit better to a girl who was once a
person, but is now a memory, and
memory consumes her,
like that night consumed her
innocence?

4. The wind doesn't whisper through
    the window, because the window is
    shut against the bitter autumn cold,
    which fits better than the summer
    breeze I pictured in my head before,
    because summer speaks of promise
    and magic,
    and neither saved me when I needed
    them most.

5. We shed clothes like a snake sheds
    skin, well one of us sheds clothes like
    a snake sheds skin.
    You can't change human nature.
    He sheds clothes like a snake sheds
    skin,
    and I shed clothes like a lamb going
    to the slaughter,
    limbs shaking like the trees trembling
    in the wind.
    Mouths smashed together between
    bouts of drunken giggles,
    a symphony of its own.

6. The bed, which is *not* covered in rose
    petals, is barely covered at all,
    as our bodies fall to the bed with the
    rest of our inhibitions.

A flailing of limbs and tongue as we
race toward the precipice,
that moment when our two bodies
would create a new universe in the
space between our flesh.

7. Through the drunken haze that has
stopped all common sense from
entering my head,
at the moment when it's the last
chance to turn back,
my brain resurfaces and I say the one
word that could stop this train-wreck
from becoming an utter catastrophe:
NO.

8. In his half-drunk mind, he hears GO,
and struggles to keep me from
running this time,
pulling me back each time I scoot
away.
I shout my 'NO' on whispered
tongues
because it's hard to shout around the
shattering in my head,
to hear above the roar that cracks the
yawning abyss open between my
thoughts.
He plows through like a wrecking
ball,
and how apt that description is,
because I was left with the battered
walls,
nothing to hold the horror at bay.

9. Tears stream down my face as he
takes what he wants,
like he has a right to my body

because he said "I love you" once
upon a time and swore he meant it.
Because alcohol and caveman don't
mix, and he thinks that because he
says "yes" it cancels out my "no".
Like I'm a piece of meat he can claim
whenever he wants to eat steak.
And as he finishes with a whispered
"I'm sorry",
I know the damage is done.
There is no coming back from it this
time.
And one last thought crosses my
mind before I fall into the first sleep
of many,
that will forever be haunted by his
ghost:
this is not how I planned it in my
head.

*-I make plans and the devil laughs.
Is that why he has your face?*

Going Under

Once the victim drops below the static
water line,
The body naturally stops breathing and
initiates breath holding
To try and protect itself.
While they struggle, the victim is still
unable to make sounds.

I want to soar.
I want to cast off these heavy chains
And fling myself into the deep, blue sky,
and fly away.
But the heavy, iron chains are fastened to
my ankles and wrists
So tightly that I can barely move.
Flying is not an option.
The chains of responsibility,
Of choices not thought through
Tighten more each day so I am chained to
where I stand.
I don't move in any direction,
Afraid of causing the chains to tighten
further.
My bones sink into the floor
Inch by inch.
If I don't break free soon, I will become a
part of this empty castle.
This pit of despair.
I look longingly out of the window and see
the world outside.
I see the sun kiss the trees with light and I
look toward the blue sky yet again.
Oh, how I long to break these chains and
fly up there.
To stretch my wings and have the sun kiss
the spots frozen like ice.
To soar above the earth, feel the breeze
caress my hair from my flushed cheeks.
I want to fly across the sky and laugh with
the moon,
dance among the stars.
I want to soar in lazy circles down to the
ground
and lay among the wildflowers in the
field.
I want the cool water from the rivers to

embrace this broken shell of who I am
and give me new life.
But, like it does every day,
the sun sinks behind the trees until I can
no longer see it.
The moon rises and the stars twinkle, and
like every night,
I'm left alone in my prison cell,
looking through my barred window and
hoping for the sun.
Each night gets longer and longer,
and I know
one day,
the sun will set and it won't return.
The hope it brings will set with it,
and I'll have only the moon for company.
And on that day, when despair finally
consumes me,
I'll look longingly toward the ebony sky
one more time,
and long to soar.
One.
More.
Time.

*-Is this why I have always loved the
night?*

It's the little things you notice first.
The extra effort you put in that's not
returned,
the touches that get fewer and farther in
between,
the sparkle that fades from the eye.

Then it's the big things.
The forgotten anniversary,
the silence of unspoken words that echo
off walls in memory,
the frigid cold on the other side of the bed.

In the end,
you're banging your hands up against a
wall
that you can see through
but no one else can see.
You're screaming at the top of your lungs
for release,
but no one hears the mute screams
on the other side of the invisible wall.

> And you're
> alone.

Everything that once meant so much is
gone.

> And you're
> alone.

**-I've never heard silence quite so loud
before**

You told me that if I ever missed you
To look at the stars
And know you were looking at them too.
But I haven't seen a star in years,
so how can we be looking up at the same
sky?

-Am I just talking to myself?

Happily ever after is a myth.
It's just a broken mirror
Made up entirely
Of pieces of my shattered heart.

-Oh how they cut deep

I am no longer
Your wagon to dump your baggage on.
I have enough suitcases
full of skeletons to weigh me down.

-Yet I can't seem to get rid of them

But here's the thing:
I'd rather break my own heart,
Shatter it into a million pieces,
Than give you the opportunity.
If I do it to myself, at least I won't
Have to reassemble the wreckage
In the wrong order.
I'll know where each shard goes,
And one won't be missing.
The piece that belonged to you.

-That is why they call me Dragon Heart

Words crest over my head and flood my
lungs,
Stealing the air that's left.
Diffidence wraps sharp talons around me
And yanks me beneath the waves.
My own personal riptide along the shore.
I kick and battle against the waves,
Struggle toward the surface,
Strive toward that sweet, single breath of
air
That waits above the waves.
Toward the light
that glitters in hazy swirls through the
murky water.
I kick.
But those dark tendrils of despair,
Pain,
And hopelessness
Wrap around my limbs,
Strangling the feeling from each one,
And drag me deep into the inky, black
depths.
Away from the waiting, sweet breath of air
That would fill my lungs and keep me
fighting.
Keep me alive.
The ebony tomb swallows me whole.
And I'm drowning.

-And the waters go deep

I wish I could make you understand.
Understand how that naive girl you loved
in the beginning
died the day my mental blocks were
annihilated by a blast
like the atomic bomb on Nagasaki.
How the brush of fingers on skin no
longer fills me with butterflies in my
stomach.
No, now that brush on skin is like a swarm
of wasps stinging where your fingers
touched.
And that smile you loved so much?
The sun that lit that smile went supernova
a long time ago,
and the light finally stopped reaching my
earth.
Dreams I laid at your feet,
trusting you with them as if you hung the
stars in the sky yourself,
and I wished on them every night.
Those stars turned out to be plastic glow
in-the-dark hopes,
falling from the ceiling as easily as the
shattered pieces of those dreams I gave to
you.
The silence stretches between us,
and the roar of it is deafening.
Each word you speak slices me open
until I am nothing but oozing cuts that
drop black ink onto white parchment.
My stains remain as I swallow your sins as
well as my own.
I am a paper doll with rips beyond repair,
a tin man without a heart.
Darkness yawns in front of me and I
welcome my racing pulse,
and visions that strangle the air from my

lungs in gasps.
I welcome the solitude created in that
empty space
where joy and laughter once grew like
roses in a garden.
It separates me from that dead, naive girl
you think me to be.
I am what you created from the start of
this.
I wish I could make you understand,
I am no longer me.

-Haven't been for a long time now

And I cut another chunk off of myself
To fit better in the glass box you put me in.
To fit better into the person you wanted
me to be.
I buried the real me under the weight of
your expectations,
so you would take more than a passing
glance.
And I'm tired.
I'm tired of failing to live up to your hopes
of what you really want.
I'm tired of pushing my soul down into
dark caverns no one will want to explore.
I'm tired of living in the gilded cage you
put me in,
locking the door so I have no choice but to
stay where you put me.
So I'm taking my crown and breaking it
into pieces,
Collecting the metal chunks and picking
the lock.
Gathering the shards of who I am,
That you broke into powdered dust,
And walking out of the cage to freedom.
Where I can breathe in deep without the
weight of you sitting on my chest.
Where I can dance with the night sky and
feel starlight kiss my skin.
Where I can walk alone and not be
reminded of you.
Of what you once meant to me.
Of the horrors that went on behind closed
doors.
Of ever loving you.
Or is loving you what I'm trying so hard to
escape?

-Scars remind me that I survived

Every breath I take is like swallowing
    seawater.
    What I mean is,
    that every time you touch me it is only to
    hold my head beneath the waves.
    Every time you look at me,
    it is only to make sure that the bubbles no
    longer break the surface.
    Each "I love you" is a chain around my
    legs that anchors me to the ocean floor.
    I cannot rise above the turbulent waters.
    I am weighed down by your insincere
    flattery.
    My tears salt the ocean,
    so it is as lifeless as the Dead Sea.
    I am drug further beneath the ice-cold
    waters by skeleton hands.
    White bone fingers crush my ankles
    like the thousands of broken promises you
    never meant to keep.
    I am the captain of a sunken ship,
    banished to the ocean floor by my vows to
    you.
    Your poisoned words are a siren's song
    that I cannot turn away from.
    I am dashed against the jagged rocks time
    and time again.
                Night after night.
    And as I open my mouth to scream, I
    swallow more seawater,
                and my death is just another
    song of the seas.

-Somehow I never get the lifeboat

Unconscious

The lack of oxygen to the body causes the
body to go into shut-down mode,
And the victim becomes unconscious.
They are motionless.
At this point, the victim will sink to
bottom of the water.

Happiness, I remember you
When I prod the scars
Remembering when I cut you
Out of my skin
Remembering how
You used to taste
Like a bitter pill
I was forced to swallow
Remembering when
I thought you were real
But you were really just
A mirage in the desert
Remembering when
I thought I felt you once
But it was just another
Sleight of hand
Happiness, I remember you
Even though I wish
I couldn't

-How it hurts to miss you so

She has fire in her veins,
Burning embers in her smile.
At the end of the day,
She's just a girl,
Who wants to watch the world burn.

-A girl on fire

You only love
Like bricks smashing through windows.
Rotting flesh dripping off of spoiled
dreams.
Like pins tearing through balloons.
Loud bangs in the silence between the
explosions of your words.
I sit at the table
Shoveling in the rotten food you feed me
All the while you call it love
And I wonder why I'm starving.
Why my bones are barely covered in skin
As your words tear through flesh and
muscle.
Why you chip away at my porcelain
facade
And I wonder why bits of me are missing.
I refuse to sit at your table anymore
A broken morsel in your mouth
That you can chew up and spit out when
you don't like my individuality.
I only love in starlight and dreams
Creating universes in between the spaces
in my flesh
Left hollow by the hit of your words
And shining light through the darkness
Until the ebony surface shines brighter
than the sun.
That's what bothers you the most
That you can't snuff out my light
With the darkness of your mouth.

-Love shouldn't hurt

        Monsters aren't found in
fairy tales.

Those thousands of beady eyes latched to
scaly skin peering out from within the
pages of books
or under your bed concealed within the
darkness.

        No, they don the flesh of men
and women like a favorite dress or suit.

Maybe that's what runs chills down your
spine—the fact that the monsters sit at the
table with you and smile over their food.

        They will get close to you and
make you trust them.

They will whisper words to you
and make you think those words weave a
safety net under the tightrope your walk.
What you don't realize is that the net is
actually a snare
and before the warning bells chime,
you are trapped.
        The pounding of your fists
will not matter in the grand scheme of
things.

You can rage against them with the voices
of a thousand men,
and it will not make a difference.
The monster will find you,
it will capture you,
and it will try to destroy you.

It will try to devour your
essence with the unlit,
                ebony grime that covers their
soul.

It will try to drag you into their hell
because you are white as snow and they
crave the clean.
It thinks that destroying you
will unlock their prison cell and let them
be free.

                What they don't realize is that
you are fire-forged.

You were molded in the very center of the
earth with a backbone of steel.

                You are a phoenix burning
everything to ash and using those ashes to
rebuild yourself.

They cannot destroy you,
for you will only come back stronger.
The grime from their hands cannot corrupt
the light of your soul.

                They cannot break you.

You were cleaved from the earth to float
among the stars,
to breathe fire on the earth and they
cannot take that from you.
They can take your innocence and rip
strips of flesh from your bones,
but they cannot destroy what you are.

You are a fire-breathing bitch-queen,

so straighten your crown and show the
monsters what happens when they play
with fire.

**-I am more than the hands that touched
my body without consent**

I am an open book,
Written in ink and Braille,
so you can use your hands
To read me
once the words fade.
Only, you can't pull your eyes away
From the world around you
Long enough to pick me up.

*-I guess you wouldn't read the Cliff-notes
either*

I held the stars in my arms when I held
you.
You were so bright,
lighting me up from within
and easily shining into my heart.
But you disappeared just as quickly,
like the moon dragging the stars behind it
in the sky
while the sun lurks out of sight waiting to
make its appearance.

You were gone.

You left me like the night leaves,
as the sun makes way for day,
and no matter how tightly I held onto you,
you wouldn't be stopped.
My arms are covered in scars
from where you burned me
as I held onto you like a lifeline
stranded on the ocean waves
in the middle of a hurricane.
I wish that things were different,
that you would be who I needed,
but that's as pointless as wishing on a star.

Like wishing on you.

You were never really good at following
through.

-God knows I still wished on you though

She trails starlight
Everywhere she goes,
Dances with the moon,
Yet you force her to the table,
And wonder why
She chokes on sunlight.

-Girl Made of Stardust 1

And so I swallowed another piece of
myself
a shattered piece of the real me
So you wouldn't feel threatened by how
bright I shine
So you could sit on your cold throne
And judge the masses
I swallowed my shine
So you could glow brighter
Each jagged edge slicing on the way down
Until I was bleeding out from within
Until each swallow dug the shards in
deeper
Until the taste of blood replaced
everything else
Until all that was left was darkness
Darkness that sets ghosts after flesh
Darkness that haunts dreams turning them
into nightmares.
You illuminate your castle,
Shining so bright that others come to bask
in your glory
And I
I dim myself down so no one can see me
Break a chunk off
And swallow another piece of myself.

-Yet I can never stay invisible

They told me to go to my happy place.
But how do I go to a place that's a person,
That person is you,
And you are gone?

-I'm still searching for you

I'm breathing.
I suck in one shallow huff of oxygen after
the other.
In.
    Out.
In.
    Out.
If I can keep the air moving in my lungs,
No one will see behind the mask I wear.
The sun kisses my face with ice-cold lips.
The summer breeze trails fire-hot caresses
to revive frozen, dead flesh.
I've no spark left in me to rage against the
night,
to claw my way through the packed earth
until my cracked and bleeding hands
break the surface.
The light in me once lit the darkness to
shimmering brilliance.
It was smothered so long ago that even its
memory is barely a flicker.
Your lips dripped honey-coated vinegar
leading me to the deep grave you dug for
me.
Still as death I lay,
an easy target for the loose soil from your
shovel to drip onto me.
The dirt got higher and higher with each
passing day
until the darkness closed in,
until silence was my only companion,
until my own voice inside my head was a
hated, miserable sound.
Numb, I am an automaton.
I move with a mechanical heart that feels
nothing.
Nothing but the silence you left in me,
with wind echoing around the empty

walls of my mind.
Nothing but the steady beat of my
mechanical heart.
Nothing but the huffs of air through my
lips that suck in grains of dirt with each
pass.
Nothing but the thud of dirt hitting earth
and flesh.
I used to envy Dorothy with her steel will
and determination,
but lately, I fancy myself the Tin-Man.
Surely it's better to live without a heart,
live without that fragile traitor that burns
pain across my flesh,
than it is to let that heart keep me captive
to be slowly buried alive.

-And so the dirt piles higher

Ictus

When the brain is deprived of oxygen,
The victim may appear as if they are
convulsing.
The victim's skin may turn blue, which is
most noticeable
Around the lips and fingernail beds.

I miss her sometimes,
The girl who used to look at the stars
And dream of a better world,
Dream of the endless possibilities
That her life could take.
I miss her,
Usually when I stare in the mirror
And watch those dreams
Vanish
Bit by bit.

-Girl Made of Stardust 2

Sometimes I stay up too late.
And in the late hours of darkness,
I feel you.
You're always there,
Just under my skin.
Always undoing all the progress I've
made,
But I can't quit you.
You're like a 30 yr habit that tastes so
good,
like the burn of whiskey down my throat.
No matter how far I run,
You're there.
And in those late night hours I wonder:
Will there ever be a time when you aren't
more than a memory?

-Memories that haunt me still

Loving you was the most exquisite form of
self-destruction.
Taking the lies that fell from your lips like
rain
And turning those shards against my wrist
Before jamming them into my heart.
Turning the kisses into poison
And the sweat from our bodies,
As we met night after night,
Into sharp knives that plunged deep.
When you finally walked away,
You didn't leave me broken like you'd
hoped.
No, by then I had already destroyed
myself.

-It doesn't hurt if you do it first

No, no—it's in the small envelope.
You can feel the tiny shards through the
thick package.
If you press too hard,
you can hear them crack like a glass
thrown against the wall.
The once-white envelope is stained pink in
places where the shards press too hard in
their paper prison.
The pieces are kept safe in the envelope,
nothing can harm them safe inside.
You ask after my heart?
You won't find it in my vulnerable chest.
No, no—it's in the small envelope.

-Look how battered it is

I took my heart from my sleeve
Fragile as the glass case I kept it in
And placed it in your hands.
You promised to take care of it
To never let it break again
And then dashed it to the ground
So carelessly
Like the promises you tossed to me.
And my porcelain heart broke
Shattered into powdered dust
So that even I couldn't put it back
together.
And yet
Yet you ask me why I can't trust you
Why I build walls so high
No one can get over
Why thorns coat the walls
Like the armor around the hole in my
chest where my heart once resided.
They say to love is to trust
To trust is to be vulnerable
To be vulnerable is to offer up yourself
Offer the pieces you wouldn't show just
anyone, but I can't do that
Not anymore
I trusted once
By giving you my heart
And you handled it so carelessly
Watched it shatter on the ground beneath
my feet
Swept up the powder
And snorted what was left of me.

-Love was always your drug of choice

If I could feel depression your way,
It would be an overcast day.
The kind of day where the sky is moody
But it's still dry enough to play.
If I could feel depression your way,
It would be a flower garden.
A few weeds to pull here and there
But blooms to brighten the darkest moods.
If I could feel depression your way,
There would be double rainbows
After every storm.
Pots of gold at each end.
Diamonds instead of raindrops.
Lessons instead of pain.
If I could feel depression your way,
I could stop this poem right here.
But here's the thing:
I don't feel depression your way.
My good days are like hurricanes, and my
bad days are even worse.
My emotions go from desert to monsoon.
There are moments when I'd do anything
to make the pain stop,
And moments when the pain is the only
thing I know to be real.
There are moments when I watch the
weeds overtake the garden.
And moments when I torch it to the
ground.
There are moments when I just want to get
out of my head.
And moments when my bed is the only
thing that keeps me from sinking into the
ground.

I'm sorry I don't feel depression the way
you want me to.
Only
I'm not sorry at all.

-Sorry, not sorry

I love you

Insincere words of hot, wet breath bounce
off the dark walls and sink into my skin.

I'm almost there.

Whispered words that slap skin against
skin like a fist.
Black tracks paint the pale parlor of my
cheeks like wounds.
Destroyed up-do, dress a wrinkled pile on
the floor, taken innocence.

I'm so sorry

Three strong words that can't piece back
the shattered world,
now in tiny shards of powdered glass
littering the floor.

Please forgive me

Too little too late.

-Yet you still haunt me

Sometimes I feel like a worn, knit sweater.
There are places on me that have been
touched so often that the wool has
decayed
and there is almost nothing left.
Other parts of me have been touched so
little
that they look white as snow
and hide that slimy darkness just beneath
the surface.

And that area just over my heart?
It is frayed with loose strings that get
caught and I start to unravel.

That's the scary part.

If you pull enough of those strings,
attached to my heart,
you will see the monster that lurks under
the wool.
The wolf in sheep's clothing.
You'll see the monster I've become
from all the touches that have made parts
of me worn,
parts of me unclean.
You'll see the savage underneath
drowning the innocent maiden to keep
water in her lungs
and stop her from screaming.
You tell me if I just let go that it'll get
better,
but it won't.
How can I make you see that it is you
pulling those strings and unraveling me?
That it's you who have put worn places in
my skin so I'm now translucent?
That it's you who have forced me to be the

wolf and not the sheep?

*-And yet you wonder why I howl at the
moon*

You're like an Indian summer in the
middle of winter.
What I mean is,
that even though you have turned my soul
to ice,
You still have the power to burn me.

-I'm still waiting for the flames to stop

The heart is a funny thing.
How it lurches in your chest.
How it rushes toward the precipice
At the first thought of love,
To fling itself over the edge
In hopes you'll catch it.
How it can still beat
When love becomes like.
When fire becomes ice.
When the warmth
Is nothing more than a memory.
How, even though it is a mangled mess,
Struggling to keep beating,
It still beats for you.
Still beats your name.
No matter how much I want to forget you,
It still beats your name.

-Though I wish it didn't

Casualty

Breathing and circulation stop.
The victim enters cardiac arrest,
the heart stops pumping blood,
and vital organs start to shut down.

Every villain is a hero in his sick, twisted
mind.
Hero worship will do that to you,
Blind you to the monster wearing the
mask of your brother.
Maybe I let you close because your armor
shined so bright in the sun.
The glare was so much like fire against my
eyes,
that I missed the rusted holes that only
your darkness revealed.
I should have paid attention,
but by the time I noticed the corrosion
leached in your armor,
revealing the villain within, it was too late
—you ensnared me.
I can still feel it, all these years later—your
body pressed against my back, smothering
my innocence as you nearly smothered me
against the mattress of your bed, your iron
grip harsh, your dark eyes violent, your
hot breath relentless in wet huffs, sickly
sweet against the back of my neck.
Did you take what you wanted?
Did it make you feel like a man?
Am I lucky that the physical barrier held
up better than the mental one you ripped
to shreds?
Did it make it easier for others years later,
when my luck finally ran out?
Was it more luck or curse that I blocked it
out for so long?
Is it luck that I see myself in the mirror,
that disgusting shell of a girl,
and not the monster
and the night
and the mattress
that took the life out of my hands?

Why do I even want you in my life?
Why do I waste a thought on what
becomes of you?
Why do I worry about the chinks in your
armor that might reveal all to princes and
peasants alike?
Why?

Why?

Why?
Why do I bother concealing your darkness
and smothering my light in the process?
You *are* a monster.
You are the villain to my story.
 You're the dragon keeping the princess in
the tower—only she's not a princess
anymore.
She traded her crown for armor, and she's
come to slay the dragon.

**-If you didn't want to be remembered as
the villain, you should have chosen to be
the hero**

Her courage was a crown that she wore
like a queen.
For years she depended on others for her
self-worth.
She needed affirmation like she needed
air.
Then, one day, she changed.
She took her hammer and metal, and
started to build.
Each disappointment,
each heartache,
went into her creation and made her suit
of armor impossible to break.
She poured everything she was into that
armor until she finally broke free of her
own chains.
When she was done, her armor was the
finest the world had ever seen.
It gleamed like fire in the sun from the
tears she'd shed during its making.
Each piece was a testament to her battle to
survive.
People tried to get close to her,
tried to find the chink in her armor,
but there was none to be found.
There were none, because that would
mean she let someone close enough to hurt
her,
and that was something she couldn't do.
She vowed that day, long ago, that no one
would ever get close enough to hurt her
again.
She placed her happiness solely on herself,
and would not be dependent on others,
never let them get close enough to try.
The wall around her heart was nearly as
impenetrable as the armor she wore.
People came and went, but it didn't matter

to her.
She couldn't care, never again.
So she polished her armor and crown day
by day,
until it gleamed so brightly it was as if the
fire that smoldered in her soul burst out
into their metal somas.
They were sheep, and she needed no one
to protect her.
And her?
She was a lone wolf.
She howled at the moon, and she would
no longer lose sleep over the opinion of
sheep.

-Fire in her veins

To love me is to love a ghost.
I haunt the walls in this shell of a body,
my windows boarded up,
the door nailed shut.
I try to keep others out to save them from
this haunting,
to keep them from the echoed moans that
rock the halls night after night.
When you say you love me,
those three words float through my body
like mist over the water
and disappear just as quickly.
I have no room for love,
no room for fate
when every breath I take is like a knife
through my lungs.
You want to save me?
You tell me to fight,
to try a little harder,
but how do I tell you that I gave up the
fight long ago?
The inky, black depths call me
and all I want to do is run away from the
light and embrace it
like I should want to embrace you.
You call my name over and over,
and I moan my pain in response
as the walls shake, the windows shatter,
and everything about me turns to dust.
You say you love me,
and I am like an apparition on the moors,
reaching through the mist and fog toward
salvation that will bring me nothing but
pain.
You can't understand why I don't feel the
same,
but I tried to warn you.
To love me is to love a ghost.

How can you be good at love
when all you know is haunting?

-So I chose specter instead of flesh

You finally did it
You broke me.
You took that final piece
And shattered it
Slamming it against the ground
So hard
That not even powder remains
And the light that was left in me
Is nothing more
Than wisps of smoke

-Darkness has always been my friend

1. We start with stars in our eyes that
   shine bright like diamonds,
   or pearls,
   or whatever gemstone metaphor you
   can attach to it.
   Those stars make up hope.
   Hope you'll get out of that one-horse
   town,
   that house that's the lead in your
   waking nightmare,
   those fists that are as quick to land
   punches,
   as the arms connected are slow to
   give hugs.

2. Then they walk in, and your heart
   stutters.
   Your world goes from black and
   white to 3D Technicolor.
   You could spend the rest of your life
   trying to describe the color of their
   eyes.
   Or how love isn't a color or a feeling,
   but a jolt to the heart you thought
   shattered.

3. Wedding bells ring, church choirs
   sing, everyone rejoicing as you step
   out into the world on their arm.
   You could float to the moon, dance
   on the stars, create life from nothing,
   as long as they're by your side.
   People tell you, "It's dangerous to
   put your happiness on someone
   else's shoulders.
   That's too much responsibility for
   any one person to hold."
   But what do they know?

They're just jealous that they don't
have what you do.
    Right?

4.   You made plans early on, but the
days keep passing and you keep
asking,
"When is it going to be my turn?"
Your Technicolor love is now just a
faded photograph left too long in the
sun.
Your one-and-only has become just
someone.
You watch the days pass faster than if
you were standing still, and yet—yet
you keep hoping.

5.   Those stars in our eyes dimmed long
ago.
One by one they're snuffed out
because life has finally done what it
set out to do.
There are no more grand adventures
on the horizon.
 All you have left is a swirl of flame
that's barely an ember.

6.   You want to die.

7.   You don't want to die.

8.   You finally want to live.

9.   You decide to live forever,
but how do you live forever when
every breath feels like razor blades
slicing deep,
and your one chance to be

remembered was gone before you
knew that's what you wanted?
So you sit down and put pen to
paper.
You write about hell because that's
all you've ever known.
You write about love because you
think you felt it long ago.
You write about truth because that's
all you know how to speak.
The ink dries.
The paper crumples.
And everything you are turns to dust
like the words you have written.
It's bittersweet, almost.
How the one thing that's killing you
Is the only thing keeping you alive.

-Will I ever find my way back?

After all this time, I was never sure
if you were the lighthouse or the storm
In the beginning you sought me out.
You lit me up
And pulled me away
From the things that could hurt me.
In the end
You were the hurricane.
You destroyed everything in your path
And I was just another casualty.
I never really knew what you were,
Only that in the end
My heart was the shattered debris you left
behind
Scattered along the rocky shore.

-Maybe I'm a siren after all

Your words slice through me like knives
and I am a shattered stained-glass window
only all my pieces are black.
You have burned my soul down so much
that I am nothing but ash,
drained down my colors until all that's left
is the pit where I once stood,
the wind picks up and I blow away.
You scream your insults at me
but your voice is as soft as a whisper,
flowing across my skin like nails on a
chalkboard.
Each word carves a groove in my skin so
deep,
the network of valleys could rival the
Grand Canyon.
I struggle to hold those black stained-glass
pieces in my hand
but they bite deep into flesh so that I have
no other choice but to let go.
I am a patchwork doll,
held together with duct tape and pure
determination
so that you cannot replace the whole of me
with the whole of what you want me to be.
I go into the night kicking and screaming
to an empty room.
No one is there to save me this time.
Nothing I do or say will stop your words
from cutting deep,
stop your whispers from changing me,
stop the colors from draining.

And your words?
They echo still,
a solid rock
smashing through my stained-
glass window.

And I shatter.

-My how those black pieces shimmer

I love the night from the inner depths of
my soul.
The way the darkness clings to the edges
of the light
like a warm embrace from a lover.
How it twists and bends around
covering everything it touches like a
familiar blanket.
The night creatures sing to a tune
only those who really feel the night in
their bones can hear.

The day comes like an enemy
stealing into the inner sanctum of the
camp.
The light burns everything it touches into
ash.
It hits my eyes and it's like acid dripping
into my skin,
into the outer shell of my soul.
It poisons everything it touches inside of
me
until almost nothing is left untouched.

And just when I think the day will snuff
out what is left of me,
the night returns,
 and I dance among the twinkling stars.

*-Shall we take a turn around the dance
floor?*

And they lived happily ever after…
That's how all the fairy tales end.
No one tells you what happens after,
Like they're afraid to tell you the truth.
No one tells you if Prince Charming still
thought Cinderella was beautiful
after she popped out a dozen kids,
or if Prince Philip thought Sleeping Beauty
was lazy
because she wanted a nap.
No one tells you if Snow White fought
with her prince
because she still hung out with the Seven
Dwarfs
and he had issues because men and
women
"can't be just friends".
No one tells you if Belle and Prince Adam
were at each other's throats
from sun up to sun down
because he acted like a beast.
So don't promise me a fairy tale.
Don't promise me "happily ever after"
when I'm still questioning the here and
now.
Don't give me a bouquet of roses and
think that you can sweep me off of my
feet.
Don't ride in on your white horse to storm
the castle and think I'll swoon.
I like my castle.
I hate the smell of roses.
I'd rather put my hopes in the happiness
of now,
rather than hang them on the hopes that
you'll still love me tomorrow.
You want to impress me?
Send me love letters about how you

couldn't sleep last night
because you thrive on the smell of my
skin,
and the scent has faded from your pillow.
Tell me how the stars pale in comparison
to the twinkle in my eye
when you watch me reading and I get to
my favorite part.
Show me that I'm your favorite part of the
day
when you trail blazing hot kisses down
my neck
like tracing your finger across my heart.
I don't want a fairy tale love.
I want that soul-burning love.
That love that keeps you up at night
because I am missing from you like a
phantom limb,
and no matter how much you reach for
me,
I'm not there.
I want a love that creates universes from a
thought.
A love that dances on steps made of
planets and a dance floor made of stars.
I want a love that's as bright as two stars
colliding—wiping out everything in its
path,
like the future I thought I wanted,
and the past I left behind.
No, don't promise me a fairy tale because
fairy tales end.
Take my hand in yours and dance with me
through the night
so you can promise me the sunrise.
I'll promise that I'll be there.
That way "happily ever after" won't make
liars out of us both.

The End...

-Is this where we live "Happily Ever After"?

Armor is a funny thing.
You hear armor, and you think of knights
Shining in the sun, sparks off of metal.
You think storming the castle,
Slaying the dragon,
Rescuing the princess.
You don't think of words turned fire,
Burning a path from me to you.
You don't think that the knight is
Actually the villain.
Or that the dragon is actually the princess,
And by storming the castle,
You have destroyed
My fortress of solitude,
Destroyed us both.
So I will be the fire-breathing dragon,
Spewing my molten-lava words like
Knives in the heart.
Only I'm not the dragon.
Not anymore.

-Though some may say otherwise

Reclamation

The act or process of reclaiming.

I sit and stare at you
My sunshine
My heart beat on the outside
I stare at you
As you grip my finger in your tiny hand
And promise that you'll conquer the world
That you'll never live through
The hell I survived
Each day passed
Fingers of sunlight
Brushing against the hand of the moon
And suddenly you weren't so small
And my promises broke
Like shattered glass
Like your favorite toy
Like the pieces of my heart
Because I'm no longer in hell alone
Now you sit down beside me
And I can't stop crying
Because you were never meant
To sit in hell beside me
You were meant to soar to the heavens
But now you have broken wings
Just
        Like
                Me

*-How I wish I could turn back time and
make you whole again*

Acknowledgments

Writing this poetry book was harder than I ever thought it would be, yet so rewarding now that it's done. I set out on this journey to put my feelings into words, to bring peace to a world that has (for the most part) been in turmoil and now I find that my mission has changed. I hope that the words that you've read will bring you peace of your own, or at least a sense of community that you are not alone. None of this would have been possible without the following people, however.

Rachel Ashworth, thanks for being an amazing friend and pushing me to write when I didn't feel like it. Thank you for reading through my drivel and helping me make it into art. I really lucked out when I married your brother.

My husband, Ben. Thank you for listening to the very rough versions of these poems and believing in me when I didn't believe in myself. Thanks for pushing me to be the best version of me.

Thank you, dear reader, for taking a walk with me on this journey. You have made the dark times well worth it.

About the Author

K.A. Moore has been writing for as long as she can remember. She took the leap and put her first book out there for the masses. A lover of all things coffee, books, and musical theatre, you can usually find her nose-deep in a book or trying to make peace with the characters in her head by writing their stories. When she's not playing referee to her four children, she's trying to keep her husky from escaping the yard and being a bad example to her other three dogs in rural Southeast, Missouri. To keep up with her adventures you can find her on the internet at:

Facebook: K.A. Moore
Twitter: @KAMooreAuthor
Instagram: @k.a.mooreauthor

Now it's your turn. Use these pages to write
your thoughts about the poems you've read
and what they mean to you, or use this blank
slate to write your own poem. Have fun, and
I hope this helps you as much as it helped
me.

Write Your Story

Write Your Story

Write Your Story

Write Your Story

Write Your Story

Write Your Story

Write Your Story

Write Your Story

Write Your Story

Write Your Story

Write Your Story

Write Your Story

www.ingramcontent.com/pod-product-compliance
Lightning Source LLC
Chambersburg PA
CBHW062230150726
47991CB00006B/2519